PASSIVE INCOME

24 WAYS TO BUILD

PASSIVE INCOME

EXTRA: Mix-ups of Passive Income

CONTENT

INTRODUCTION

24 WAYS TO CREATE PASSIVE INCOME

1 / Videos & Photographs

2 / AIRBNB

3 / Online Courses

4 / Create a Personal Website - Blog

5 / Sell Your Used Things

6 / Dropshipping

7 / Influencer on Instagram

8 / Affiliate Marketing

9 / Stock Exchange

10 / Print Shop On-Demand

11 / Sell Websites and Online Stores

12 / eBooks

13 / Create an APP (Application)

14 / Funnels - Funnels

15 / Create a YouTube channel

17 / jingles or Audio Tracks

18 / Crowdfunding

19 / Coaching

20 / Rent Your Car

21 / Index Funds

22 / Peer To Peer Loans

23 / Real Estate (REIT)

24 / Network Marketing

EXTRA

Mix-ups of Passive Income

Lack of Belief

Lack of Action

Without Discipline, nothing happens

Introduction

Passive or residual income is the type of money that is earned or generated without having to spend time to continue making it. That is, it's produced automatically without you having to be there daily working it. And that is the dream of any person, so deny it, to make money while you sleep, to make money while you travel, to make money while you play or recreate, that is anyone's real dream because if you achieve that you can get any other dream because 99% of dreams or things you want are bought with money, that's the truth.

However, most people, to be a little more specific, 95% of the people on the planet know another way to make money, and it's a product of work, that is, a job, and that type of payment you really don't want. That money is called "Linear Money" if you work you earn money, but you work you don't make money, and that is the type of money that you earn today? Have you thought about if something happens to you? If you get sick? If you have an accident and become disabled? If you get fired as work? Have you thought about your retirement? What will you live on when you are an old man and don't have the strength and energy to continue working? Who is going to pay your bills? Because a friend pension is something that makes you sad because it's a pittance in any country in the world, and that's what passive money is for, to be free as soon as possible and to ensure a dignified old age, where you don't have to think about it. Fear about money because you already solved it by building assets that generate passive or residual money, money that works for you, me, without meeting schedule, you enter, you live life.

And that is what you will learn in this book; you will be able to learn the source in several ways how to generate passive money, money that you can produce from home, without meeting schedules, without bosses and planning your vacations when you really feel like taking them.

So, start to read carefully and without stopping every one of the details that I present here so you can begin your journey towards economic independence.

24 Ways to Create Passive Income

1 / Videos & Photographs

Audiovisual content is an important source of income today because everything moves through social networks, people around the world are more aware of news, fashion, events, and entertainment than anything else; the news and magazine channels have been digitized, and there are also more powerful sources even now such as TWITTER, INSTAGRAM, FACEBOOK, and YouTube, and the invasion happens through your eyes the average person loses more than 10 hours a week in on social networks because they get caught by entertaining videos or attractive photos one after another. They can't stop watching them, and this can help you generate passive income. You can create your account in any of these media and constantly upload content to increase your followers to reach the point of starting to capitalize.

You can also record videos from your phone about news, happenings, daily life, events, demonstrations, protests, festivals and political conferences, press conferences, conventions and shows and sell it to companies related to these sources of information, you can professionalize this occupation and buy equipment quality to improve your content and also have a better edition.

But if you want this to be your passive job, you can also attend public events such as protests, demonstrations and festivals, record videos, and sell them to the media and online press.

You can also create a Blog to upload the content there and promote your blog to the interested media so that they have immediate access to your videos and photos, and they can offer to buy you the information to have exclusivity.

And there's another way: sell your photos and videos on web pages that are dedicated to selling this type of material to millions of marketers worldwide who need content to create their designs or advertising campaigns, and I leave you some pages here;

-PEXELS
-ISTOCKPHOTO
-SHUTTERSTOCK
-CLIPSTOCK
-PIXABAY

2/ AIRBNB

The applications (APPs) came to globalize businesses and make everyone's life more comfortable and more straightforward, and to give us more possibilities or options to generate income, and that is the case of AIRBNB that allows you to upload properties without a greater protocol to put them in rent, but wait, I know you think that you don't have several houses out there available and don't know what to do with them (hehehehehe), you can also through AIRBNB rent a room in your house, or you can build in your property an additional space or annex for this purpose with independent access.

I tell you that on one occasion I was planning to go on a trip to the beach (I love the beach) and I was looking for a house on AIRBNB (we would go a large group). I found for rent a couple of "hammocks" known elsewhere as "*chinchorros*", these were at the back of a house that had an exit to the sea, it also had a beautiful view, and they were perfect for a romantic night or a spectacular sunset looking at the horizon, so I called my wife to tell her, and when I came back to show them, and at They had booked (incredible), AIRBNB represents a tough blow to the hotel industry in many countries, including the United States, even in some areas it's forbidden to rent your property through AIRBNB.

AIRBNB is an excellent option to generate a residual or passive income that practically does not require much effort, just upload the promotional photos on the website, review and sign the conditions agreement, keep the space clean, and attractive to guests, and maintain the place, so it doesn't deteriorate, and that's easier than working at a McDonald's. The best thing is that you don't have to commit to a long-term rental so that you can stop this activity at any time.

3/ Online Courses

The world is focused on online, virtual, or internet, as it sounds better to you. People don't want to go to a physical place or a classroom to receive information if they can do it from home, sitting at the table of the dining room, or in your room, or the park, or in the pool, without spending gas, or mileage of your vehicle, or wear, and even less time in queues, traffic, and traffic lights.

A very good option is to think of a topic that you are passionate about that you like, a topic that you feel comfortable with, that you have some knowledge that you can take advantage of preparing material, and I will tell you; It does not have to be very sophisticated or technical.

There are practical, and straightforward sites where you can see this type of material, but you can also create your blog or website. I assure you that there will be hundreds, and thousands of people interested in your tips, and tricks, you just have to find the topic, and the Niche,, and the great secret here is to provoke the massive traffic that circulates through your page.

There are other sites already created, and with more significant user traffic (already insured) for this world of online courses that have become a multimillion-dollar industry, and I leave you here:

-DOMESTIKA
-CLICKBANK
-HOTMART
-UDEMY

This is a perfect way to generate passive income because you only have to do the course once, wait for the approval from the page, and voila, wait for the money to start reaching your account.

And wait a moment, these sites have a very interesting way of operating, and that is that their maximum potential is affiliate marketing that makes your online courses exposed daily, and thousands of people who will offer your courses in exchange for a commission percentage. You can do the same instead of creating a course from scratch.

4/ Create a Personal Website – Blog

You can create a web page from scratch, it's simple, and you start from the most basic by shaping your page. You should think of an initial topic, and begin to shape it, upload content, photos, images, videos, and copywriting, and once you start to get known, and get organic traffic, you can begin connecting or linking a variety of things/tools to your website to monetize it, such as advertising, affiliate LINKs either of products, services or courses related to your topics. Still, you can also sell your products, either your creation, and resale of some brands that you recommend from experience that you are demonstrating on the subject.

This can become a constant source of passive income, so much so that many, if not most, or almost all or all Digital Marketing specialists have pages of this type.

Here the advantage is free imagination because you can practically create a website of absolutely anything you can think of because there's something very safe, human diversity is impressive, and here you can unleash your imagination and creativity. The best of all is that you will not have anyone controlling you or respecting any rule, the page is yours, and you control and command it, it's something independent, here your success is in your hands, and you can create your brand and your style, and That is something very sold today, people love that which is represented by someone, that which is presented by its creator, by someone normal, someone like you and me who was able to build something and achieve success, That, the human is much sought after today, and the public applauds creativity.

5/ Sell Your Used Things

Definitely, most people are compulsive buyers, almost everyone having or without money ends up buying a lot of things that will accumulate year after year, and that will leave them unused, including many people even end up renting container spaces to save those things that are already in your way, because yes, most people are accumulators and the best solution for that isn't to spend more money on renting spaces to store all that, the best idea is to sell all of that.

Get rid of all those things that no longer serve you, and that sometimes even generate more expenses. So get to work and start doing a thorough checkup on your home and start making a list of all that; Books, clothes, kitchen utensils, garden things, chairs, sofa, ornaments, pictures, shoes, magazines, collections of sports cards, soccer world cup albums, glasses, caps, hats, beach articles, tools and also articles electronic, all that, and if you have one of those rented spaces to store things that I'm sure you don't remember many of, the best amount in your car and leave at full speed until you reach the place, open the container, mount everything in the car, take an inventory and put everything on the internet to sell it as soon as possible and earn good extra money, this friend is straightforward to do and is also a swift and practical alternative, and best of all, guess what? There are a lot of people out there waiting for a good second-hand deal.

I leave you a list of some of these sites because there are a lot;

-Amazon

-eBay

-Offer Up

-FaceBook MarketPlace

-Mercado Libre

-WallaPop

-Vibbo

-OLX

-Segundalia

-Mi Trastero

Why can you make this business a source of passive income? Because there are large companies that receive many items in return that can no longer be repackaged and return them with a defect, and these companies sell these lots on these same pages. Their pages, and what you should do is buy these lots, put them up for sale on the pages already mentioned and hire someone to take your orders and make deliveries, this way, you can systematize this business model.

6/ Dropshipping

This is one of the methods of sale by internet or electronic commerce most used nowadays, since it basically consists of creating a web page to sell products that you don't manufacture or produce and that you don't keep in stock either, so it consists of a Triangulation of retail product sales shipments where the retailer does not store the goods in his inventory, but takes and passes the order (and shipping details) to the wholesaler or manufacturer, who dispatches the products directly to the end customer or consumer

Triangulation can be on a product or service order and occurs when a retailer, who typically sells in small quantities to the general public, takes the order for one or more units of the product or service and passes all this detail on automatic to the manufacturer or wholesaler who supplies or dispatches from his establishment or warehouse directly to the buyer.

The shipment can be in "masked package," which means that it does not include the sender, so as not to identify the retailer that it's not the source of dispatch. In some cases, the address or identification of both is placed, or failing that the retailer receives the appointment of "distributor or authorized service center."

The retailer, that is, you, receives a commission or percentage on each sale made, taking advantage of the margin between the wholesale and retail prices. Said price will always be previously fixed in a "Triangulation Contract" on the conditions of sale.

Dropshipping is one of the most profitable ways to generate more income.

This is a method that can be systematized and left on autopilot since everything can be synchronized from your website, and I leave below a list of platforms where you can start your first dropshipping business;

-Volusion

-Shopify

-Squarespace Online Store

-WixStore

-Square Online Store

-BigCommerce

-WordPress Ecommerce

-WooCommerce

7/ Instagram Influencer

Social Marketing is revolutionizing the planet, and it's that all the advertising agencies on the planet realized that people don't want to buy by seeing a stranger who uses or consumes it, that does not interest the public, nowadays The "Y" generation and the Millennial generation care more about buying something than being a humanized brand, that is, they want to see someone behind the brand, someone in the flesh, a real human being, not an actor or actress, and there are the influencers, ordinary people who became famous and popular for merely being charismatic or mounting videos or photos of things they like or amuse, or for merely showing themselves as authentic. That to people today is so exciting that this market has become huge and powerful, catapulting hundreds if not thousands of young people or people to become Millionaires at a much faster speed than any traditional entrepreneur and guess what? Without investment, more than your image, photos or videos, and of course; Time spent generating enough content to generate traffic that leads to a considerable amount of followers, where today more than followers, the most important thing is "Engagement" (interaction of followers with publications; "Likes" and Comments).

All this power of influence makes large and small companies prefer to invest in advertising through influencers than in advertising paid for by television or radio, and this can represent a lot of money depending on the sponsor.

How to start?

Open an Instagram account and start generating content, interact with users and increase your followers, choose a topic and gas as much as possible to stay attached to that niche, and best of all, there's something for everyone; travel, fashion, underwear, swimsuits, shoes, suits, food, diets, exercises, nutrition, reading, books, cooking, astrology, sex, humor, politics, tarot, religion, pets, etc.

You don't need to start selling on Instagram absolutely nothing, calm they will write to you, and they will look for you to offer you money to publish or promote their products or services, and you can expose your audience to that information.

8/ Affiliate Marketing

Affiliate marketing is referring by all digital means LINKs of different products or services of the diversity of online companies earning a percentage commission on the indicated value. It's one of the most popular ways to earn passive income today.

The most striking thing about affiliate marketing is that practically all large companies or brands have an affiliate program.

For example, Shopify can give commissions through its affiliate program of up to $ 2000, which is excellent. However, it's an exception since most offer commissions of 10% or less. On the other hand, online course websites can offer in most of their packages up to 50% commission per course referred and sold.

The best way to generate passive income with affiliate marketing is to create a blog and monetize it with a variety of tools, including those with affiliate LINKs. This works very well because you have total and absolute control over your blog, you can also use your social networks and expose all your traffic and audience to the products and services offered, of course, this will work when your content is related to LINKs of affiliates that you are offering, that is, regarding the recommended products or services, and you could recommend them because you use them and say they are good or effective.

I leave you some of the best companies in this market, which are the ones that move the most traffic and are the most recognized in their different areas:

-Amazon

-Shopify

-Hotmart

-ClickBank

9/ Stock Exchange

Investing in shares of the stock market is one of the best types of passive or residual income that can exist. The only downside is that you will need to have investment capital.

I also recommend you run away from all Network Marketing or MLM companies that may offer you to develop or invest in the stock market through these schemes because, in reality, this market does not work that way. You will realize that in reality what they offer you is a study system to prepare or teach to invest and it happens that in most cases (99%) who teaches you isn't an expert and is very far from Wall Street, simply It's someone who registered a couple of months before you but simply speaks well and believes what he says (hehehehehehe!), so the recommendation is that you look for a broker, and in most banks you will find this service, in fact there are banks specialized in this subject and where you put the money and they play with it, and literally they play with it, since the world of the stock market is a kind of casino where you enter with a bet and you can win or lose and this can happen very quickly, that is, you can earn a lot of money in a matter of seconds or minutes and in other cases in a few hours, but the same way you can lose everything, and that's what these are about, these markets are aggressive in most cases and it's because they depend on a lot of factors that can be very difficult to define and that is why you have to look for specialists who know more about placements and short and long-term behavior, therefore based on this it's always better to start on the stock market with stable stocks, which don't generate many profits or dividends but are safer, have moderate but more stable growths, and these stocks are those that come from government agencies, funds government, army, insurance, health, etc., and apart from these markets we have Gold.

I recommend you study hard, take stock and placement courses, finance, and economics courses so that you can better understand the terminology and terms and to be able to understand your broker and demand or discuss some decisions until maybe one day you feel ready to take control.

I leave you some of the most recognized brokerage houses in the United States, of which almost all can be contacted online and start investing without having to be in the United States;

-TD Ameritrade

-Etrade

-OptionHouse

-TradeKing

-Scottrade

10/ Print On Demand Shop

Nowadays most people are tired of buying their certain brands, nowadays most people prefer to buy their things, and when I say their things I mean practically everything, from brands created by entrepreneurs and the reason for that is that there's a lot but a lot of talent that went asleep or hidden for years until the internet age came. It evolved through a diversity of websites where all these innovative artists, creators, inventors, designers, and small entrepreneurs can expose all his creations and let his extraordinary creativity fly.

Become one of those talented people and exploit, and capitalize on those qualities and talents, because there are several websites dedicated to just that. Better yet, most of these online companies are large factories that operate on the internet and lend you all its infrastructure so that you assemble your designs in an almost infinite variety of objects and articles and against demand; t-shirts, mugs, plates, jackets, pictures, caps, hats, pens, glasses, notebooks, notebooks, ties, slippers, t-shirts, bracelets, bracelets, necklaces, earrings, rings, belts, decals, and everything you can think of and I'm sure your imagination is already flying.

This is a great source of passive income once you have made a brand, a style, and start having clients, and I can tell you that these pages have high traffic.

I leave you here some of the best pages;

-Printful

-Printify

-Imprimir Aura

-Conseguido

-Teespring

-Spreadshirt

-Redbubble

-Zazzle

-SunFrog

11/ Sell Websites And Online Stores

Here is a detail, you must know how to program, but if you don't know you can learn, so you could create passive income by selling websites and online stores.

This way of generating passive income requires a little more effort since you must have the prior technical knowledge or acquire it through courses and practice. Also, after creating your websites and/or virtual stores you must check that it works, that is, practically the game is to sell an operating business and billing, which takes time; however, many people are willing to pay for those virtual companies that behave like assets because once they begin to practically bill the traffic they keep up with advertising or sales funnels that take people to the website. There the process is automated, of course you have previously programmed it that way.

Here it's a matter of finding a winning product to put it in front of a niche and start billing.

Also, instead of selling the website or the virtual store you can rent or rent it and earn a percentage of the sales that are being made.

Thus you earn less but you get a monthly income, of course the first case would be a direct sale and a single profit for each site or website sold, and here in this 2nd modality your client may not have the capital to buy the website because they only have or have capital to invest in the merchandise they must buy to cover sales. I would also like to try the store and profitability before moving on to the purchasing step.

And if you already have a site like this or are thinking about starting to create it, here is a platform that allows you to put it up for sale, because I'm sure you were wondering: And after creating the site and putting it into operation, who the hell I sell it to him? And here comes the answer;

Exchange Marketplace, the Shopify exchange market.

12/ eBooks

Many people love to write but have never
dedicated themselves to it because they think
that becoming a famous writer is a very
complicated matter, and perhaps that was
many years ago. Still, today the internet once
again broke that paradigm. Because you can
write a book about absolutely what you can
think of without having to print it and go
through hundreds of publishers who have to
read your book and wait weeks for a queue of
hundreds of books to be evaluated so that in

the end they tell you not to. they are interested in your book, because today isn't a problem. You can let your imagination run wild, write an eBook on the topic of your preference, choose something that you are passionate about so you can flow, and edit it yourself, next step, publish it on your social networks, publish it through FaceBook or Instagram, or Better yet, sign up for the Amazon Kindle program and have access to millions of readers eager to find literary works on various subjects by unknown authors, as well as You.

So, if you like to write, go ahead, go ahead, it's easy, and there are infinite endless niches because there's something for everyone. And I'm going to tell you something, there are thousands of new writers sitting in front of a LapTop writing at home, in the parks, on the subway, on the beach or anywhere making money through this very lucrative method, which It's a million dollar industry. It's super accessible since it's just writing your book that does not have to be a 500-page literary work, it can merely be a good writing with good content of 30 pages, but come here, in Amazon for example enters a market of 150 million subscribers in 72 hours maximum after being approved by the review team, and uploading that manuscript can take 10 minutes after having it finished along with the cover.

Oh, by the way, this is an eBook, I like to write, when I start I feel like I can't stop and the ideas flow one after another, and if it doesn't work to monetize I wouldn't, I would look for something else to put my time and make money passive.

And there's something extraordinary, if you write an eBook and see that it's having a good reception, you can translate it into any language for just about $ 25 (We are talking about 35 pages) on service platforms like the ones we already saw (example: Fiverr), Imagine the reach that you can have through the internet and on platforms with as much breadth and traffic as Amazon, Aliexpress, eBay, Wish, among others.

13/ Create an APP

It could be said, literally, that today the world is dominated and controlled through APPs, AH! ... wait! You don't believe me? So, look at your smartphone, by the way, guess why they call it that? Smartphone!!! Here is the answer; because it's full of applications that allow you to use your phone for pathetically anything, this is impressive. Let's see, there are applications for; exercise, measure your weight, turn your phone into a magnifying glass, GPS, compasses, calculators, personal income and expenditure management, play, access to all banks, Forex, food deliveries, package deliveries, restaurants, Astronomy, channels from movies and tv series, finance, video editing, music, translators to all languages, travel agencies, tourism, flashlights, social networks, economics, news, radio stations, Ecommerce, chats, videoconferences, calendar, creation and design, and anything that goes through your head, bone, this is an invitation to put your imagination to fly.

I'm going with a statistic; Every day around 5,000 applications are created, of which 90% of them die in the initial phase of exposure to the public, that is, in their period of testing and acceptance, but yes, if you create one that is welcomed in the market, you get rich in a matter of months.

What do you have to do to create an application?

The first thing is to sit down and think about some social problem, something that has to do with the population, and find a practical solution through a simple application that everyone can download to their phones with just a click, and then view it. and start capitalizing.

You must prepare in programming if you want to develop it yourself, or failing that, hire a programming company to help you with the development of it, yes, make sure you sign confidentiality contracts. For that you need a lawyer to I can protect your rights of "Intellectual Property" because otherwise, I assure you, no, I swear, it's more I promise you, they will steal the idea. They will develop it for them to become millionaires.

So here what matters is the creative detail and putting action into the development of the system because we are facing one of the most powerful sources of passive or residual income in recent times, so much so that practically, if your business does not have an APP you are insignificant to the commercial world, what's more, you are harmless, they don't pose any threat, it could be said that you don't exist, at that level we are talking, and it's that I can assure that the entire world or 95% of the civilized planet that we know today will be managed or controlled through applications for the simple reason that almost 95% have access to a Smartphone with internet and consequently what you put on those cell phones it will translate into being in the hands of all the people who have one at a single click, and that is a winning idea that today is already a reality that every day is more potentiated, has even transformed the reality of many spaces physicists and the way of working and earning money for many people.

And now let's talk about some applications that today make the lives of thousands more comfortable and have made their owners super millionaires:

Amazon, eCommerce system where you can buy almost anything, and just like this application, there are other similar ones; eBay, OfferUp, OLX, Alibaba, AliExpress, among others.

UBER, an urban transport system that replaced 95% traditional taxis, as well as; LYFT, CABIFY, and DIDI, among others.

TURO, allows you to rent your car while you aren't using it.

AIR B&B allows you to rent a house, property, or a room.

DoorDash, delivery of restaurant meals at home, as well as; UBEReat and Postmate among the popular.

AMAZON Flex, to deliver packages at home from the Amazon company.

PayPal, for electronic money transfer.

WhatsApp, chat for communications, as well as Telegram, WeChat, Line, and MeetMe as the best known.

Instagram, social network like Facebook, Snapchat, Twitter, Tik Tok, and LinkedIn with the most traffic.

And the invitation is to create yours because this is a passive income.

14/ Funnels

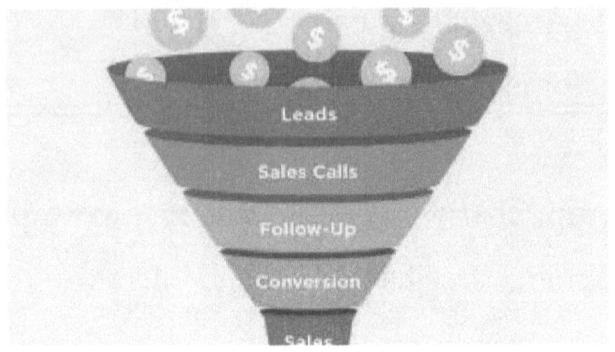

This marketing strategy was super complicated to develop a long time ago, you had to know a lot about programming, creating and designing web pages and integrating tools, and this can be very overwhelming and overwhelming for those of us who aren't so technological, however, today that isn't like that, Because many companies have developed very intuitive software for creating funnels that anyone without programming knowledge, even a child, can do it because it's practically like putting together a puzzle. These systems are full of tutorials that explain step by step everything there's. What to do to build the funnel?

But what is a funnel, and what can we do with it?

A Funnel is a digital marketing tool that allows you to advertise a product or service through the internet, and consists of an advertisement launched through a post or video through social networks or search engines, and they are also added as links in web pages of Blogs, news, companies, and once the interested party is exposed to advertising and clicks, the funnel system is activated since it goes to a page called Capture Page where generally the client leaves his data, almost always name, surname and email and perhaps his telephone number, and immediately goes to a second page where he is shown a little more information presenting the product and making an offer, whose offer always is improved on another page making it increasingly irresistible to complete the sale, and if by chance the client does not buy and tries to leave the page, a message called PopUp appears, indicating that they expect there to be an even better offer, with the intention of lowering the price a little more or offering some additional service product in half the price or increasing the discount, and if by chance the sale isn't completed then that customer will be chased through your email for days, in some extreme cases up to 3 months of daily mail or intermediaries presented and remembering the product or service, almost always offering some things for free, perhaps an eBook, on other occasions a free course or a sample, all this to continue attracting the customer, And last. Still, not least, the most sophisticated will chase you through social networks for any web page you visit during the next 30 days this is impressive, one of the most used and powerful marketing strategies in recent times.

And your friend can use this tool in several ways, leaving you here 2 options;

1/ Build a funnel to capture leads (Prospects), and I'll give you an example; Observe in your community some clinics or perhaps some medical centers, aesthetic clinics, Spas or GYM, create a funnel to promote any of these businesses and collect data from those interested, and when you have optimized the funnel and are generating a good amount of daily leads see and offer the funnel to the owners of these businesses as an advertising tool and attract potential customers, and you know what? Do you know how much you can charge? grab your seat, because you can be charging for each of these funnel about $ 1000 to $ 2500 per month, and this is good news because right now I have 3 funnels of this type for which I am charging $ 1500 for each one. I take build each of them around 5 days, and to get the same residual buying real estate product you would have to buy a property of at least $ 150,000.00 for the cheapest.

2/ You can look for a product, analyze it, do a market study, maybe do some reviews on

Amazon, eBay and Google to determine a product that is highly received and in demand, and yes, build a sales funnel, which was the origin reason for this marketing tool.

I leave you here the most popular and best platforms for the construction of funnels:

-Clickfunnel

-Sumo

-HubSpot

-Smartfunnel

-Wishpond

-Builderall

Funnels behave like passive systems, however, they tend to stop giving results after several months, since people get bored of seeing the same thing and it's long production periods of up to 6 months of results where you only sit to receive the money in your account.

15/ Create a YouTube Channel

Google bought Youtube, and since then there has been an incredibly exponential growth in the display of content in video format; there were even many people who started earning reasonable amounts of money overnight, and others became millionaires. Although today It's not so easy, the opportunity is still present, and new emerging YouTubers always appear. And I know! You would love to become a YouTuber, become a millionaire by uploading videos to the network, videos without much sense but entertaining, just enough that they have an audience and that can be any niche, as strange as it may seem, you can become a YouTuber by uploading videos of your tattoos every time you get one, or black humor jokes, or just bad jokes, but it can also be about jokes, improvised songs, or also deceiving people by uploading videos revealing magic secrets and hidden strategies to make money online that nobody wants you to discover. Still, a Youtuber comes and is showing it to you with more than 500 thousand views. If you check well, you find hundreds of other YouTubers in different languages revealing the same secrets and magic formulas (hehehehehe!), but guess what? IT WORKS!

And if it's true that there's more and more competition on YouTube, it's also true that it's the second content search engine on the Internet after Google. It's expected that in a concise time, it will become the first, and that translates into a very high potential. economic, and that this tool is in a second stage of growth, so look for your surfboard and ride the wave.

This method will hardly make you free for life, but surely you can generate an interesting residual, and it can also be a lot of fun, so if you have charisma, don't waste it because the cameras are waiting for you and YouTube wants to pay for it.

Surely you know or have heard of a millionaire Youtuber, however, they aren't the majority they are very few, perhaps many earn a few thousand dollars, which is great, and here is the payment relationship that applies YouTube that will depend on the content, since it varies between humor, children, technology, politics, gossip, etc.

We are talking about an interval of $ 3 to $ 5 per 1000 views.

Being the best paid at the moment, the contents related to Forex, Health video games and curiosities.

Let's get accounts!

You have a channel of 100,000 subscribers, which will probably take 1-2 years to build.

You upload one video per week that gets 50,000 views and YouTube pays you the minimum of $ 3 depending on your content. We would be talking about $ 150 a month for that video, and if you upload 4 videos a month with that average of views we would be talking about $ 600 per month, but residual.

However, apart from the money you can receive directly from YouTube, you can also monetize your channel by receiving sponsorship from companies that make toys, or diapers, or children's clothing, or energy drinks, or tools, wow! , video game developers, travel agencies, and for you to count.

I recommend that you start this project as soon as possible because you can build it and it will take several months to grow, but I assure you that you are going to have fun.

We can mention as a last thing that, if YouTube simply causes you to close your channel and it closes and that's it, so be very careful to avoid making a mistake uploading inappropriate content because YouTube does not mess with games.

16/ Audiobooks

I love it, I love it, I love this way of generating money, and I love it so much because it's based on giving added value, creating something and monetizing it, but when I say create, I mean that you should let your imagination run wild, your ability creative, innovative, discover your muse and take advantage of something that you master, some knowledge, some special skill on which you can generate content, write a manuscript and prepare it to be able to record it in audiobook format and start earning money for royalties.

I confess to you that I have not yet dabbled directly with audiobooks. Still, I am already doing the pertinent research to bring all my eBooks to this type of edition since it's very profitable, as much as audiobooks, in fact there's a huge niche of people who prefer 1000 times listening to an audiobook than sitting down to read a book, for the simple reason that in today's hectic and troubled world people who have normal jobs are increasingly flooded with working hours and go from full time to part-time. time and after leaving that part-time they go another (hehehehehehe!), you will say that I exaggerate. Still, many people in the big metropolises work up to 16 hours a day and that is incredible, because if you put the time of transfer to the workplace, the time to get ready and eat, you have maybe 3 hours left and they use them to sleep, I don't think they use them to read, but guess what? While driving to your job site or on the subway, or even on the job site, you can wear headphones and Voilà!! There they begin to listen to an audiobook, and most likely it's an audiobook on personal finances, investments, how to make money from home, how to generate passive income, etc., precisely to see if they find a way out of their rat career and begin to decrease hours of those part-times that are killing them.

I leave you here some platforms where to expose your audiobooks to monetize them;

-Audible

-Audioteka

-Audiolibros

-Audiobooks

-Ivoxx

-Moon Reader

-iTunes

Now, to create your audiobooks I recommend these two platforms;

-AX
-eSpeak

Finally, this is a great and very elegant way to generate passive income, literally royalties for intellectual property on your audio-recorded works. While others listen and delight you sit down to see how the money enters your account, yes, This will work for you if you create quality content that is interesting and well-crafted.

17/ *jingles* or Audio Tracks

This is another elegant way to generate royalties because it consists of creating your audio tracks where you will have their intellectual property. Here again you must look for your muse, your creative capacity, your genius, and take all your talent and monetize it, of course It's that this source of income isn't so easy to create, it's more specialized, and I leave it to unknown artists who can make a lot of money through this medium.

So if you know how to play a musical instrument you can create some of your original audio tracks, or you can also search for songs that are playing a lot, the most popular ones and you can create or play music from your instrument; piano, organ. Keyboard, flute, guitar, saxophone, clarinet, trumpet, accordion, violin (this is one of the favorites for audio listeners) and then mount it on one of the platforms that work for this, which I leave you here;

-Audio Socket

-Sound Cloud

-Song Freedom

Hey, come here! you don't have to be a dedicated musician either, I have several friends who are sound engineers and create music tracks from computers. These melodies are also highly sought after by young people, especially by the Millennial generation who love techno music, electronics etc. artificially created.

18/ Crowdfunding

This is also known as Loan and Collective Financing Platforms, which work through financial or other donations, to finance a particular project in exchange for rewards, altruistic participations, shares or interest on the contributed capital.

This is an easy and fast way to generate passive income, which does not end up being extremely high. However, logically the more capital you contribute the more money received in return. Of course, the advantage here is that these sites have algorithms that help reduce the risk even though you are talking about a project that may fail, before starting the exposition of the project it has already been evaluated by a team of experts who have carried out a market study, analyzed the possible scenarios and the projection capitalist of the project in question.

Sure, here you must have capital, but I expose the option because I find it viable, interesting, to generate passive income. Some people are just looking to put their money to work for them. They don't have time to create new things because they are already very involved in other businesses that occupy their time but want to multiply their capital, because of something if we are sure, in the bank they will not produce anything in your favor, rather the bankers will take your money and use it to make investments and earn much but much money.

OK! We are going to mention some of these platforms;

-Prestadero
-Kubo Financiero
-Briq

Please, before placing your money in some of these systems, check that these companies are affiliated with the Association of Collective Funding Platforms (AFICO).

19/ Coaching

Coaching isn't easy, you must be prepared in some specific area, and you must be good if you intend to make money with this method, you must also have patience because you must make a name accompanied by a good reputation in growth that will be what in the end will bring you clientele. Please, don't go into this field if you don't have studies, preparation and/or experience, because you are going to look very bad. Not only that but you will lose time and money others who seek to grow in some area, whether personal or business, that is, don't become one more charlatan of those who abound today in social networks saying that they know a lot about something and know absolutely nothing, because today almost anyone with a few followers already believes in coaching (hehehehehe!).

Another thing to take into account in this profession is that it has a difficult scale, since you must be very creative to be able to take this method to a group system that allows you to monetize massively, since most coaching end up working with a few clients already. that they don't personalize the accompaniment because each case is particular. In that case you must be good but outstanding to be able to charge high rates and be profitable for you. And the fact is that most of your clients are going to want a 1 to 1 face-to-face accompaniment.

Now if you sit down to elaborate a good strategic plan that you can digitize and create a group format, then you hit the nail on the head.

Now, once the whole system is assembled, I assure you that it will be very gratifying to see how you help other people to earn a lot of money, arranging their business, relationships and personal affairs, and at the same time earn money for that, we can say that it's a profession full of purpose.

Here the cornerstone is really to lead your clients to achieve measurable results, and that will depend on all the others, because with one or a group happy with their goals achieved, the rain of clients will arrive eager for you to empty all your wisdom and guidance on them.

To promote this project, you must start by establishing a digital marketing strategy through social networks such as FaceBook, Instagram and Youtube as the main ones, as well as a Blog where prospects can interact and to drive interested traffic in your services. It does not have to be something so elaborate, on top of that what counts is that it's valuable content, that would be the honey for your ants.

Here the groups must be reduced so that you can provide a good experience, and that leads you to demand and prepare yourself more and more, but you can charge a good figure if you demonstrate your capabilities, which will help you earn good income in the medium term.

Something positive and interesting is that places like the United States are very fashionable. The topic of coaching is very popular with figures such as Tony Robbins (Personal Growth), Robert Kiyosaki (Investments and Real Estate) and Grant Cardone (Business and Sales) , which has promoted the concept worldwide, with more and more coaching figures appearing and many countries in Latin America mainly, as well as in Spain and the United Kingdom.

If you are good you will have practically no competition, on the other hand, the risk is almost nil since the investment is meager, and from the point where you have developed your training or coaching program, all you have to do is wait for the prospects while you are advertising to expand and make yourself known, taking advantage of radio programs, community aid, free advice, in the church of your community, social clubs, charity clubs, etc.

20/ Rent out your Car

Here is a simple one, rent your car, and I am going to give you several safe ideas;

UBER, you can rent your vehicle to drivers or drivers to use your vehicle while you aren't using it, for example, when you are at work, at nights when you sleep and on weekends that you will not leave home. Now if you have investment capital then you can buy multiple cars and do the same full time for these drivers. You could be charging an average of $ 50 per day for each standard vehicle, and thus build a systematized business with little supervision and producing passive income. , that then at the end of the useful life of the car you can sell it and get capital to buy a new one and keep renewing and expanding your fleet and at the same time increasing your income flow.

HYRECAR, this application allows you to rent your vehicle but in a safer way even than the previous one because everything is managed through an already created system. You only incorporate the cars to the same where they are monitored, and the same application keeps your vehicles available for different drivers that enter the app looking for cars to work, which in turn can be used to operate in various applications such as Instacart, UBEReats, Postmate, Doordash and

AmazonFlex. Here the idea is also to create a fleet of vehicles to increase the flow of income more and more.

TURO, this application is very practical because it allows you to systematically and safer the initial idea of renting your vehicle to do UBER, however, in this case the concept changes because here you make your vehicle available while you aren't using it (when you are at work, weekends or at night), and when a TURO user needs a car, then he turns on his application where the closest available vehicles will appear, then simply goes to the car where he takes it and uses it to do so. you want, go to another place, supermarket, the beach, etc., with the condition of returning it in the maximum time limit established by the owner, in other words, You!

In all these cases you already know that the initial idea is to make extra money by renting your vehicle. The second idea is to make this a business by acquiring several cars to create a fleet and generate a greater volume of income, which will require a little more effort, basically administrative and supervisory, of course. At the same time, you build a structure that allows you to hire a person to be in charge of maintenance and to review the fleet daily and the different operational details that come with having a fleet of vehicles that require oil change and filter, tires, fluids, cleaning, etc.

21/ Index Funds

This is a good way to generate passive income, probably one of the best, or perhaps the best of all because you put your money in and that's it! done, wait, unlike TRADING where you must buy and sell shares daily, which isn't residual money at all because each operation depends on you. Incidentally, it's a daily dedication because your profit lies in the profit of each sale positive earned, here you don't need to do anything, you just leave your money working for you. You just leave the money there and forget about their movements, no matter if stocks go up or down.

Here the investment is made in the market in general, not in a specific company, and this favors you enormously because you don't have to worry about details such as choosing specific investments, balancing your portfolio or knowing when to sell or buy, because your investment portfolio will be operating on autopilot.

The great advantage here is that the operating expenses are minimal because the services of research analysts aren't needed and you must regularly pay a broker or stock analyst to select your investments.

This is a very good choice if you have your thoughts in the long term, of course the utility isn't overwhelming, the percentages of profit are usually low but very safe, and the more money you put to work for you in this scheme the more the money will be what will you get in return.

We are talking about an average of 5% for the lowest shares and 15% for the highest, where you can enter with about $ 1000 but with no subsequent investment time, which turns out to be very easy because what you need is capital investment, being this always my option when investing in the stock market. The one that I recommend, in fact it's here where I recommend to go putting all the money of utility obtained from other businesses.

22/ Peer To Peer Loans

Now, this straightforward form brings with it details that you must legally handle to insure your money, you have to analyze the risks very carefully in each particular case, that is, with each person or client, and the recommendation is that the money you are going to use to start this business model it's not a capital that you need immediately or in the short term.

The direct person-to-person loan is also managed for small businesses, in both cases it will almost always be when neither of these two figures qualifies for a traditional or regular loan at a bank.

I must make several recommendations, and the first of them is to thoroughly investigate the profiles of the clients to whom you intend to lend the money, you should also distribute the loans among several people to minimize the risks before an unscrupulous potential client who refuses to pay or widely delay the installment periods and total principal of the loan. On the other hand, I also recommend consulting with an attorney and/or accountant to write a basic and simple but legal document that supports you and commits the client to executing and honoring the loan, this will also help you not to incur any irregularity before the law that can later be used against you, or in any case and the main reason is for any client who refuses to pay.

Finally, definitively this isn't my best option and the one I recommend the most, in fact I don't like it very much. However, I apply it today after many bitter experiences so that it can be a real headache, remember that these Clients did not qualify for a traditional loan at a bank where they could have obtained a much better interest. Yet, they came to you who is probably handling an interest rate of double or triple or sometimes 4 and 5 times more than a bank, obviously Because you don't manage the large funds and capital that a financial institution manages.

Ah, of course, you need investment capital.

23/ Real Estate (REIT)

The expression REIT comes from the English "Real Estate Investment Trust", which is understood as Reliable Investments in Real Estate, and this is the absolute best alternative to invest in the real estate sector passively.

This Alternative consists of not looking for properties on their own, which can take a long time to investigate not only in the legal part of the property but also in its structural and maintenance conditions, since the memory of the owners or sellers often hide damage behind SheetRock, putty and paint, such as broken pipes and termites, among other things. At the same time, here we avoid all this and go to a mutual fund for real estate projects.

We are talking about huge entities that are generally listed on the stock exchange and whose main objective is that small and medium investors can participate in large real estate projects that would otherwise be impossible to access because they would be millions and millions of dollars in most of the cases.

You can work these funds one at a time, that is, you choose one, you put your money there and that would be it, of course you need advice for this. My recommendation is to find a broker that can support this and support you in the operation with their experience, but here security is very, very high since these projects have been evaluated by a team of experts from all points of view, they have projections of 10 years, perhaps 20 years and sometimes up to 30 years in the future with analyzes of all kinds, Therefore, when it has been decided to start the project, its profitability is more than assured, which provides many benefits and a lot of liquidity, making this option a very attractive and better alternative than traditional investment in real estate.

Something very practical is that you don't get tied up, in almost all cases you can sell your fund whenever you want and the value can increase very quickly in a short time. It's because professionals manage them with a lot of experience who know exactly what they do and how to make that money yield, so you only have to get good advice from your broker to study the benefits of the fund and the exit options and then put your investment and see how it grows.

24/ Network Marketing

"Network Marketing emerges today as the most powerful distribution method and the most attractive business model in the new economy".

- From the book The New Professionals by Doctor Charles King, Doctor of Business Administration from Harvard University, and Professor of Marketing at the University of Illinois, Chicago.

Yes, as you are reading it, if you want to build an empire online, and become a billionaire and even a billionaire, Network Marketing is the best option, but not only that, it's the most powerful for the simple reason that you can start with practically nothing. investment and have access to a huge company that operates in many countries and markets who are responsible for absolutely everything; production, guarantees, storage, returns, dispatches, call center, taxes, legality, education, incentive trips and infrastructure. We are talking about a global business where you can earn in various currencies and travel the world knowing cultures and developing leadership and influence, and really impact lives. If this catches your attention then you are in the right place, because these experiences can also be highly rewarding.

But I'm not the one saying it, all these books say it;

The Business Of The 21St Century
Robert Kiyosaki

How to Build a Multi-Level Money Machine: The Science of Network Marketing
Randy Gage

The WAVE 4 Way to Building Your Downline
Richard Poe

My Business of People, 20 Years Later
Luke Mills

Go Pro - 7 Steps to Becoming a Network Marketing Professional
Eric Worre

Your First Year in Network Marketing: Overcome Your Fears, Experience Success, and Achieve Your Dreams!
Mark Yarnell

And I can name many more where they will affirm that this business model will take over the world economy in the coming years, since any human being willing to excel through training will be able to create their own independent business that will function as a kind of franchise.

But here I clarify a little more the panorama.

What is Network Marketing?

Network Marketing is defined as how the manufacturer introduces his products in the market in the form of "Business Opportunity ".

Network Marketing is a form of distribution of products and services, directly from the manufacturer to the final consumer, without intermediaries, facilitating through personal consumption and by recommendations to others, generating continuous profits.

What are the reasons that make us decide to be a Networker?

Along the way we have met many lawyers, doctors, managers, architects, small business owners, who abandon "success" and don't look back. Thousands of people of all kinds who recover dreams and illusions, all have joined to the ranks of the new professionals.

Many of them have decided to embrace an industry that they once laughed at, mocked, and vowed never to make contact with.

But what exactly is Network Marketing?

It's the low-cost industry that invites you to develop your own business and obtain potentially high income working from home and on your own schedule.

You get immediate income through the sale (which today you can do 100% online) and significant residual income by reaching products and services directly to consumers and inviting other people to do the same.

Known in the past as multilevel marketing and historically despised for having been considered a pyramid scheme for unsuspecting and manipulative people, it emerges today as the most powerful distribution method, and the most attractive business model of the new economy, today you can get it under the names of Social Commerce and Social Marketing.

I leave you here the list of the first 10 and the most powerful:

You can see that AMWAY doubles the profit of its closest competitor and the 2nd in the list, that is to say, really, it has no competition, therefore, if you are going to start in this business model because enter with any other if you can enter with the first, number 1.

However, maybe you like a particular line of products, perhaps you identify with a market; diet, makeup, health, energizers, vegans, organic, essential oils, etc. You just have to be clear that here it will require a lot of work, focus, dedication and hours, but you can do it in your free time spaces, you can see it as part-time, and build something giant in a matter of 3 to 5 years.

I wish you success in your adventure, but it excites me to know that I am not the only one who resists being a slave to the system and burning the best years of his life at the mercy of a job, with a schedule and a boss who end up getting rich. and you further and further from your dreams. Entrepreneurship is the way!

EXTRA

Mix-ups of Passive Income

If you already got here then you already realized that there's another way of living where you can create your lifestyle by creating your world, your environment and your source of income, in struggling to find a job and die of boredom doing the same year after a year for a salary that will not grow until you grow old and die, probably without a penny in your pocket, old and sick, and also very lonely for sure.

By creating passive income, you can live without a schedule required by a boss and work from anywhere in the world while your income continues to be produced day after day.

But, here comes the great "But", there are very few who manage to turn that dream into reality, because it depends on several intangible factors that all reside in your mind and on the power you may have to dominate them because in reality they are all disciplinary factors, habits you can create or remove, and that my friend depends on you, and that's where those mix-ups come from, let's start;

Lack of Belief

Everything that looks like earning money from the internet and that looks like residual income sounds like a mirage, a

Chinese tale and a scam, and here many already give up because they prefer money earned with the sweat of their forehead day after day, but yes, "yes they pay me work ", and that is linear money, so these people aren't made to live the emotion of building passive income.

And it's that these types of people have a hard time seeing that the effort you are putting today will not be immediately rewarded, this will be paid after several attempts, and it can be many until you get the right mechanism according to the type of passive income you are looking to seek utility.

As logical as every one of the strategies described here may seem, the truth is that most people don't believe they are capable of creating and developing them, and here a lot are left out of the game, so they are waiting for you. a long working day for about 40 years.

I recommend these books;

Believe It to Achieve It: Overcome Your Doubts, Let Go of the Past, and Unlock Your Full Potential
Brian Tracy

Unlimited Power : The New Science Of Personal Achievement
Tony Robbins

Lack of Action

Here we find a group of brave and dreamers who if they believe they can build passive income but never finish launching any project, are very afraid of failing and spend hours thinking about details to start some passive income adventure but paralyzed by the fear of just think that they may neglect the job they have and lose it because they are thinking about financial freedom, running out of bread and cheese. Since no idea that occurs to them seems like an absolute winning idea, they stay there, as dreamers.

Others in this category spend months designing the perfect plan and spend months adjusting details, precisely because they don't finish visualizing or clicking on their winning idea.

I give you something, don't wait for the winning idea, what I recommend is to make attempts, it begins, that's all, you try, you must take steps forward, along the way you can make adjustments, otherwise you will never start, and only like this You will be able to learn, because in everything I have done none but none of my ideas have worked for me in the first one, all of them have produced me after months of making adjustments testing niches, investing time and money, and in other cases it simply has not worked and I've had to move on to other ideas.

you have to create several sources of residual income and the intention is to be able always to keep making money in various markets; if oil goes down, if a hurricane comes, if the cost of medicine goes up, if the stock market plummets, if real estate falls apart, if a war breaks out in the Middle East, if anything happens, it doesn't matter because you you have your sources of passive income diversified.

So long hours without sleep await you, much to think about, many attempts ahead, struggling with frustration, perhaps with the ridicule of your friends, percent, many of them will look for you to borrow money once they see you earn money , traveling and having a good quality of life, and never think that creating sources of passive income is blowing and bottle-making or rubbing Aladdin's lamp and waiting for the genie to appear and fulfill all your wishes and suddenly overnight. Tomorrow you will get rich.

See you at the world's airports.

Get moving and act.

Without Discipline nothing happens

We go for the third group, which believes it and has also decided to take action and take its first risky steps, but does not have the necessary Discipline to keep persisting and make attempts after attempts, adjustments after adjustments to achieve the desired result, simply he starts, makes several attempts and gives up because he has a hard time fighting against frustration.

Let me tell you that Discipline is a significant factor of success. You should definitely know that to succeed you must decide to get up every day to make your ideas work, think about how to make it work, shape it, make attempts, don't give up, put your thinking 100% positive and shout to the universe that you will not give up until the objective is surrendered at your feet. Of course, here too a lot roll and return to their jobs running before they can lose it.

I recommend several books that can help you with different factors of Discipline and perseverance;

Shoe Dog: A Memoir by the Creator of Nike
Phil Knight

The Monk Who Sold His Ferrari: A Fable About Fulfilling Your Dreams & Reaching Your Destiny
Robin Sharman

Think and Grow Rich
Napoleon Hill

Think Big: Make It Happen in Business and Life
Donald Trump

The Power of Focus: What the World's Greatest Achievers Know about The Secret to Financial Freedom & Success
Jack Canfild

Creating Passive Income Really Isn't Easy

This is so, creating passive income isn't easy, all the strategies described here require time and dedication, and in some cases also require capital investment, so you must create your sources of passive income without haste, without stress and with maturity, otherwise you will feel suffocated and you will surrender without having won a single dollar before.

You can never place all your hopes in a source of passive income that you are designing, in fact if you study the great millionaires you will realize that as they grow in capital they are always looking for where to move and create new sources of passive income to diversify their investments and alternatives, that is why